Goods

HEINLE
CENGAGE Learning

Young & Son
Global, Inc.
A YBM COMPANY

What do you buy at the market?

Contents

grow

farm

make

factory

buy

sell

Goods are everywhere.
We use goods every day.

People use computers.

People use paper and pencils.

People eat fruit.

People drink milk.

What are goods?

Where does corn come from?
First, a farmer grows corn on a farm.
Next, the farmer sends the corn
to a market.
Then, we buy the corn.
Things that farmers grow are goods.

1 Growing

2 Sending

3 Buying

9

Where does a bicycle come from?
First, a worker makes a bicycle
in a factory.
Next, the factory sends the bicycle
to a store.
Then, we buy the bicycle.
Things that workers make are goods.

1 Making

2 Sending

3 Buying

Fruits are goods.
Toys are goods, too.

She sells clothes at the store.

He sells food at the market.

Goods are things that people grow or make to sell.

How do these become goods?

corn

bicycle

Goods! Goods!

Goods! Goods! Goods! Goods!
We grow goods. We make goods.
We sell goods. We buy goods.
We all use goods every day!

Goods! Goods! Goods! Goods!
We grow goods. We make goods.
We sell goods. We buy goods.
We all use goods every day!

Index